June Flew

by Lauren Quillin
illustrated by Andy San Diego

Practice Decodable 73

McGraw Hill Education

Bothell, WA • Chicago, IL • Columbus, OH • New York, NY

MHEonline.com

Send all inquiries to:
McGraw-Hill Education
8787 Orion Place
Columbus, OH 43240

ISBN: 978-0-02-145066-4
MHID: 0-02-145066-8

Printed in China

8 9 10 11 12 DSS 27 26 25 24 23

This was June's first plane ride. She felt thrilled. The plane looked like a long tube.

The crew helped June. They told June the flying rules. June grew very excited.

The plane started slowly. Then it went faster. In seconds, it flew!

June had fun on the flight. June read and played tunes. She even saw the news.

June looked down a lot. She spotted cities, roads, and farms. June drew some of what she spotted.

The big plane landed. When June saw Gramps, she smiled.

"I flew! I flew!" she said.